When The Well Runs Totally & Completely Dry

PRESCHOOL RECIPES, FINGERPLAYS, AND GAMES

Created By
Gloria Wheat Thompson

© 1996 Broadman & Holman Publishers

What do you do with those "in-between" times?

Fingerplays, cooking, and games are wonderful development and reinforcement tools for preschoolers. But coming up with fresh ideas week after week is challenging. What do you do if:

- The itsy bitsy spider refuses to go up the spout one more time?
- Your idea of a recipe is "Take 2 slices of bread, spread with peanut butter"?
- "Duck, Duck, Goose" fails to generate the excitement that it did the previous 6 weeks in a row?

So you are thirsting for fresh ideas but the old well of ideas is dry as a bone!

What's a teacher to do?

Your satisfying drink of water is here. This book is overflowing with activities to quench your thirst for ideas. And the activities are designed to reinforce spiritual truths and teachings for your preschoolers.

So, go ahead. Take a sip, then settle back and gulp down the soothing flow of refreshing ideas.

Ahhhhh!

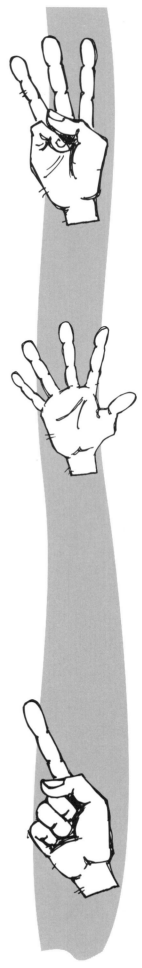

FINGERPLAYS

Fingerplays provide a strong, visual tool for reinforcing teaching concepts or for using small and large muscle groups. Preschoolers continue to delight in these, even after many repetitions. Fingerplays can be used to teach a specific concept or just as a fun time filler. Within each category on the following pages, you will find some Bible thoughts which these fingerplays can reinforce.

NATURE

Bible Thoughts

God made the animals. Genesis 1:25
Everything God made was very good. Genesis 1:31
God made the fish. Genesis 1:21
God made the trees. Genesis 1:11
God sends the spring rain. Jeremiah 5:24
God takes care of the birds. Matthew 6:26

FIVE LITTLE CHICK-A-DEES
(Hold up fingers to represent numbers)

Five little chick-a-dees sitting in a door,
One flew away and then there were four.
Four little chick-a-dees sitting in a tree,
One flew away and then there were three.
Three little chick-a-dees looking at you,
One flew away and then there were two.
Two little chick-a-dees sitting in the sun,
One flew away and then there was one.
One little chick-a-dee sitting all alone,
One flew away and then there was none.

BOA CONSTRICTOR
I'm being swallowed by a Boa Constrictor,
And I don't like it one bit!!
Oh no, he swallowed my toe,
Oh gee he's up to my knee,
Oh my, he's up to my thigh,
Oh fiddle, he's up to my middle,
Oh heck, he's up to my neck,
Oh dread! HE SWALLOWED MY _____!!
GURGLE! GURGLE! TICKLE! TICKLE! BURP!!!

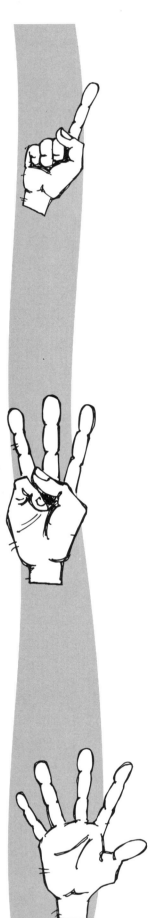
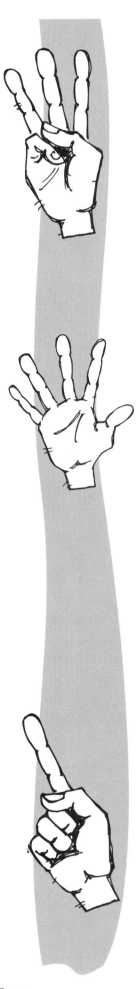

TWO MOTHER PIGS

Two mother pigs lived in a pen. (two thumbs up)
Each had four babies and that made ten. (hold up four fingers on each hand)
These four babies were black and white, (right hand four fingers)
These four babies were as black as night. (left hand four fingers)
All eight babies just loved to play,
They rolled and rolled in the mud all day, (roll hands)
When night time came they huddled in a heap, (fold hands tightly together)
And squealed and squealed until they went to sleep. (hands together next to face)

WIGGLE WORM

Wiggly was a wee worm, (wiggle 1st finger on either·hand)
Who wiggled everywhere. (wiggle finger around through the air)
Let's see where Wiggly went... (open eyes wide)
It started at my toes, (wiggle finger slowly up from the toes)
Wiggled all the way up to my nose! (wiggle finger up to nose)
Then wiggled back down without a peep, (have the finger worm wiggle back down)
Fell into my pocket, and went to sleep. (pretend to go into a pocket)

KITTENS

Little kittens standing in a row, (hold up all 10 fingers)
They bow their heads to the children so; (bend fingers down)
They run to the left and they run to the right, (fingers run left and then right)
They stand up and stretch, with all their might; (fingers tall)
Along comes a dog who wants some fun—
Meow! Meow!
Just see those kittens run. (put hands behind back)

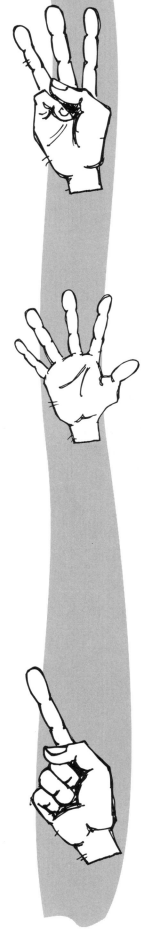

LITTLE BROWN POTATOES

Little brown potatoes (make circle with thumbs and pointer fingers)
Growing in the ground (make fists and hold together)
Covered up with soft, brown earth,
Making not a sound. (hold pointer finger to lips)

Down came the rain (wiggle fingers downward)
One stormy summer day,
The underground potatoes (make fist and hold together)
Slept the day away.

Out came the sun (make large circle with arms over head)
The farmer came out, too,
He dug up those potatoes (open fist)
to give to me and you. (motion to give one to a child and to keep one)

HERE'S A BEEHIVE

Here is a beehive. (make a beehive with fist)
Where are the bees? (look around for bees)
Hiding inside (try to see inside the beehive)
Where nobody sees!
Soon they come creeping
Out of the hive (open fist slowly)
One, two, three, four, five! (extend fingers one at a time)
Buzz, buzz, buzz! (make fingers flutter around)

LITTLE ROBIN

Little Robin Redbreast
Sat upon a rail (fingers in fist, thumb up, little finger out)
Niddle noddle went his head (make thumb nod)
And wibble wobble went his tail. (make little finger wobble)

TWO TALL TELEGRAPH POLES

Two tall telegraph poles, (pointer fingers up)
Across them a wire is strung. (second fingers outstretched to touch between pointer fingers)
Two little birds hopped on, (thumbs to position against "wire."
And swung, and swung, and swung. (sway arms back and forth from body)

FIVE LITTLE CHIPMUNKS
(Hold up fingers to represent the numbers)

One little chipmunk, without anything to do,
Found a friend to play with and then there were two.
Two little chipmunks, happy as could be,
Had a little visitor and then there were three.
Three little chipmunks, going to the store,
Met another playmate, and then there were four.
Four little chipmunks, going for a drive,
Shared their candy with a friend and then there were five.

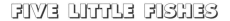

FIVE LITTLE FISHES

Five little fish, (hold up one hand)
Swimming in a pool, (hand makes swimming motion)
First one said, (hold up one finger)
The pool is cool, (arms together-shiver)
Second one said, (hold up second finger)
The pool is deep, (hands spread showing distance)
Third one said, (hold up third finger)
I'd like to sleep, (hands together next to face)
Fourth one said, (hold up fourth finger)
I'll float and dip, (arms outstretch, head back)
Fifth one said, (hold up fifth finger)
I see a ship, (hand over eyes)
A fisherman's boat comes along,
The line goes over with a splash! (throw line over)
Away the little fish swam with a dash. (make swimming motion)

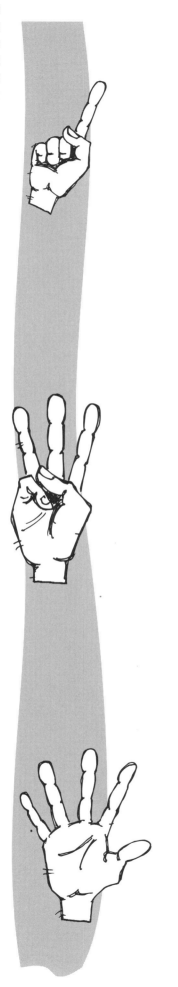

THE LITTLE TURTLE

There was a little turtle, (closed fist, one finger peeking out)
Who lived in a box. (finger in closed fist)
He swam in the puddles, (swimming motion)
He climbed over the rocks. (climbing motion)
He snapped at a mosquito, (snapping motion)
He snapped at a flea, (snapping motion)
He snapped at a minnow, (snapping motion)
And he snapped at me. (snapping motion)
He caught the mosquito, (closed fist)
He caught the flea, (closed fist)
He caught the minnow, (closed fist)
But he didn't catch me! (point to self)

TURTLES

(Hand in a fist, hold up one finger at a time)

One little turtle feeling so blue;
Along came another, now there are two.
Two little turtle on their way to tea;
Along came another, now there are three.
Three little turtle going to the store;
Along came another, now there are four.
Four little turtles going for a drive;
Along came another, now there are five.

WHAT THE ANIMALS DO

We'll hop, hop, hop, like a bunny, (hop on two feet)
And run, run, run, like a dog. (run around)
We'll walk, walk, walk, like an elephant, (arm hanging down
while walking)
And jump, jump, jump like a frog. (stoop down and hop)
We'll swim, swim, swim, like a goldfish, (hands together,
swimming motion)
And fly, fly, fly, like a bird. (fly arms like a bird)
We'll sit right down and fold our hands, (fold hands)
And say not a single word. (finger on lips)

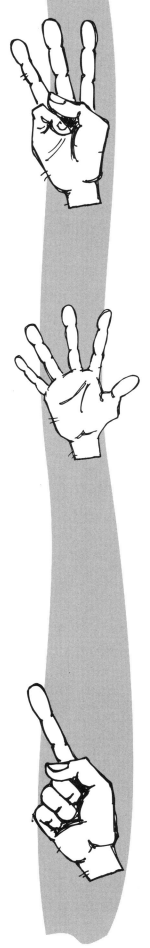

THE TREE

I am a tree, and I'm so tall, (stretch very tall)
That you can't see my top at all.
My branches sway with the breeze, (sway from side to side)
And gently toss my pretty leaves.
In the autumn when the hard winds blow,
My leaves flutter down to the ground below.(flutter fingers down)

ON THE APPLE TREE

Away up high in the apple tree, (point up)
Two red apples smiled at me, (make circles with fingers)
I shook that tree as hard as I could, (pretend to shake tree)
Down came those apples and mmmmmm were they good! (rub tummy)

HOUSES

Here is a nest for the robin; (cup both hands)
Here is a hive for the bees; (fist together)
Here is a hole for the bunny; (finger and thumb make a circle)
And here is a house for ME! (fingertips together to form a roof)

TEN FLUFFY CHICKENS

Five eggs and five eggs, (hold up fingers for numbers)
That makes ten.
Sitting on top is the mother hen. (fold one hand over the other)
Crackle, crackle, crackle, (wiggle fingers-opening slowly)
What do I see?
Ten fluffy chickens, (wiggle open fingers)
As yellow as can be.

SEASONAL

Bible Thoughts

Jesus was born. Matthew 2:1
God loves us and sent His Son. 1 John 4:10
Jesus loves you. John 15:12
God made the winter. Psalm 74:17
God made the trees. Genesis 1:11

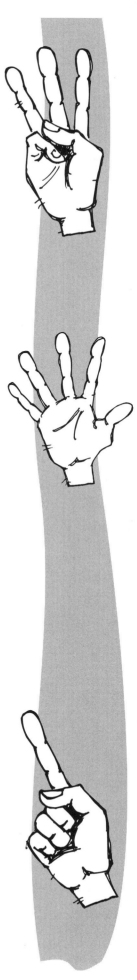

CHRISTMAS IS HERE

Here is the wreath that hangs on the door,   (make circle with arms overhead)
Here is the fir tree that stands on the floor,   (triangle with thumbs and forefingers)
Here is the book from which carols are sung,   (sides of hands touching in book position)
Here is the mantel from which stockings are hung,   (place one bent arm over the other bent arm in front of body.
Drop one arm like a hanging stocking)
Here is the chimney that Santa comes down,   (make rectangle with thumbs as base and fingers for sides)
Here is the snow that covers the town,   (finger flutter down)
Here is the box in which is hid,   (close right fist with thumb inside and place left hand on top)
A Jack that pops up, when you open the lid.   (lift left hand up and pop out thumb)

CHILDREN'S CHRISTMAS TREE

Here's the children's Christmas tree, (make triangle with thumbs for base and fingers for peak)
Standing straight and tall,
Here's the pot to put it in,   (cup hands together)
So it will not fall,
Here are two balls, bright and beautiful,   (make circles with thumb and index fingers of each hand)
One ball - two balls - see? (hold up to see)
And two tall candles red!   (hold index fingers up straight for candles)
To trim our Christmas tree. (repeat triangle)

FIVE LITTLE BELLS
(use five bells)

Five little bells hanging in a row, (five children hold bells in a row)
The first one said, "Ring me slow," (first bell rung slowly)
The second one said, "Ring me fast," (second bell rung fast)
The third one said, "Ring me last," (third bell rings)
The fourth one said, "I'm like a chime," (fourth bell rings)
The fifth one said, "Ring me at Christmas time." (fifth bell rings then all the bells ring together)

EASTER RABBITS

(motions: hold up fingers to represent numbers)

Five Easter rabbits standing by the door,
One hopped away and then there are four.
Four Easter rabbits sitting near a tree,
One hopped away, and then there were three.
Three Easter rabbits looking at you,
One hopped away and then there were two.
Two Easter rabbits enjoying the sun,
One hopped away, and then there was one.
One Easter rabbit sitting all alone,
He hopped away, and then there were none!

I AM A SEED

I am a seed in the earth below, (crouch down)
Down came the rain, to make me grow; (fingers like rain)
Up, up, up, tall as can be, (start to rise)
Now I am a big, big tree. (stand tall and spread arms)

FIVE LITTLE SNOWMEN

Five little snowmen, happy and bright, (hold up five fingers)
First one said, "What a beautiful sight," (hole up first finger)
Second one said, We'll never have tears," (hold up second finger)
Third one said, "We'll stay here for years." (hold up third finger)
Fourth one said, "But what will happen in May?"(hold up fourth finger)
Fifth one said, "Look! We're melting away." (hold up fifth finger)

PEOPLE

Bible Thoughts

Love your father and mother. Exodus 20:12
We work together. 1 Corinthians 3:9
We are helpers. 2 Corinthians 1:24
Help one another. Galatians 5:13
God helps us. Psalm 46:1
Work with your hands. I Thessalonians 4:11
God cares for you. 1 Peter 5:7

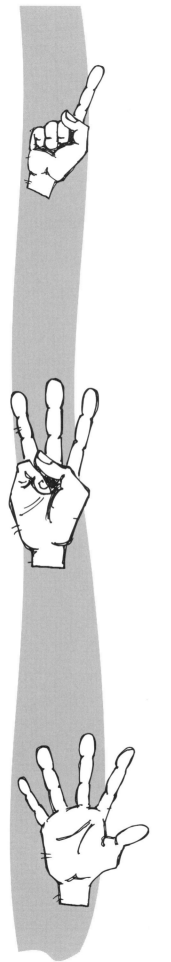

MISS POLLY HAD A DOLLY

Miss Polly had a dolly, (make cradle with arms)
Who was sick, sick, sick,
She called for the doctor, (pretend phoning)
To come quick, quick, quick.

The doctor came, (swing bag)
With his bag and his hat, (point to hat)
He rapped on the door, (pretend to knock)
With a rat-a-tat-tat.

He looked at the dolly, (hold dolly in hand)
And he shook his head, (shake head)
He said, "Miss Polly,
Put her right to bed."

And he wrote on his paper, (pretend to write)
for a pill, pill, pill,
And he said, "I'll be back in the morning,
With a bill, bill, bill. (Wave good-bye)

JOHNNY WORKS WITH ONE HAMMER

Johnny works with one hammer,
One hammer, one hammer. (pound one fist)
Johnny works with two hammers,
Two hammers, two hammers, (pound two fist)
Johnny works with three hammers,
Three hammers, three hammers. (pound two fist, and one foot)
Johnny works with four hammers,
Four hammers, four hammers. (pound two fist and two feet)
Johnny works with five hammers,
Five hammers, five hammers. (pound two fist, two feet, and head)
Johnny works with five hammers,
And then he falls asleep. (hands together against cheek, eyes closed)

TEN LITTLE FIREMEN

Ten little firemen, sleeping in a row, (pretend to be sleeping)
Ding dong! goes the bell, (wave bell in the air)
Down the pole they go, (pretend to slide down the pole)
Jumping on the engine, (pretend to jump on the firetruck)
OH! OH! OH!
Putting out the fire, (pretend to hold the hose)
Then go home so slow.
And back to bed again - all in a row. (pretend to be sleeping)

FAMILY HELPERS

This little boy washes the dishes; (pretend to wash dishes)
This little girl cleaned her room; (pretend to clean the room)
This little boy took out the trash; (pretend to take out the trash)
This little girl used the broom; (pretend to sweep)
This little boy said, "Yeah!, yeah!, yeah!"
I'll be a helper, too!"
(You may choose to use the fingers as in "this little piggy"
instead of doing the action)

GRANDMOTHER'S GLASSES

Here are grandmother's glasses; (circle each eye with fingers)
Here is grandmother's hat. (hands in peak on top of head)
This is the way she folds her hands; (fold hands)
And lays them in her lap. (lay hands in lap)

MY FAMILY

Finger people are such fun,
Let us count them one by one.
First come Father, (pointer finger)
Next come Mother, (middle finger)
And this tall one is the brother, (ring finger)
Here is Sister with her doll, (little finger)
Here is Baby, last of all. (thumb)
Now we'll count them, just to see,
How many are in our family,
One, two, three, four, and five.

THINGS

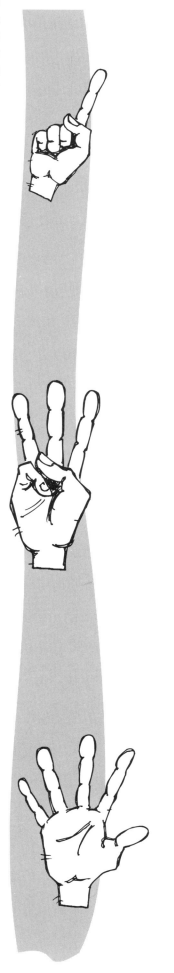

Bible Thoughts

The Bible is useful for teaching us how to live. 2 Timothy 3:16
God gives us things to enjoy. 1 Timothy 6:17
God made the world. Acts 17:24
Look at the wonderful things God made. Job 37:14
Give thanks to the Lord. Psalm 107:1
Everything God made is beautiful. Ecclesiastes 3:11

I'M A ROCKET

I'm a rocket, (crouch down)
Pointing to the moon, (point up with fingertips)
4—-3—-2—-1—-,
Blast off! Zoom! (child springs up and jumps into the air)

HERE'S A BALL

Here's a ball, (make circle with thumb and forefinger)
And here's a ball, (make a circle with thumbs and forefingers)
And a great big ball I see, (make circle with arms and hands)
Can you count them? Are you ready?
One, two, three.

SAFETY

Stop! Look! Listen!
Before you cross the street.
Use your eyes, (point to eyes)
Use your ears, (point to ears)
Then use your feet.

SIGNAL LIGHT

When I see the red light,
I know that I must stop.
The yellow one means wait,
It's never on the top.
The next one signals go,
And it is always green.
NOTE: Make red, yellow, and green circles. Let three of the children hold them up when the color is said.

ENGINE

Here is an engine, (hold up one hand)
That runs on its track. (hold other arm out for the track and let the engine run down it)
It whistle "toot—toot," (hand pulls string for whistle)
And then it runs back. (engine runs back on track)

JACK-IN-THE-BOX

Jack-in-the-box, all shut up tight (make fist with thumb inside)
Not a breath of air, not a peep of light.
How tired he must be, all in a hump;
Now release him, and let him jump. (make thumb jump up).

MYSELF

Bible Thoughts

God made me. Psalm 119:73
I am wonderfully made. Psalm 139:14
God gave us ears to hear. Proverbs 20:12
God gave us eyes to see. Proverbs 20:12
Jesus grew and became strong. Luke 2:40
Work with your hands. 1 Thessalonians 4:11
I thank God. 2 Timothy 1:3

BIRTHDAY FUN

This is _____. (child's name)
It's his/her birthday today.
He's/she's _____ year old, so they say.
Let's count his age as we clap our hands,
To let him/her know we think he's/she's grand.
1, 2, 3, 4, 5. (count and clap to age of child)

CAN YOU WIGGLE

Can you wiggle a very small part of you? (wiggle fingers)
Can you wiggle a big part of you? (wiggle whole body)
Can you wiggle a part of you below the waist?(wiggle hips and legs)
Can you wiggle a part of you above the waist? (wiggle upper body)
Can you lie on your stomach and wiggle like a worm? (lie down and wiggle)

EXERCISE FUN

Reach high, touch the sky, (reach up high)
See the birds flying by. (flap arms)
Bend low, touch your toes, (reach down and touch toes)
Wobble as the old duck goes. (hold ankles and walk)

FUN WITH HANDS

Roll, roll, roll your hands as slowly as can be;
Roll, roll, roll your hands; Do it now with me.
Roll, roll, roll your hands; as fast as fast can be;
Roll, roll, roll your hands; Do it now with me.

Other verses:
Clap, clap, clap your hands.....
Shake, shake, shake your hands.....
Stamp, stamp, stamp your feet.....

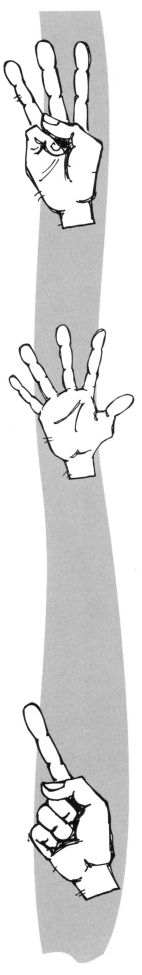

HANDS

Hands on your hips, (hands on hips)
Hands on your knees, (hands on knees)
Now put them behind you if you please! (hands behind)
Then on your nose, (hands on nose)
Touch your eyes, (hands touch eyes)
Then touch your toes. (touch toes)
Hold your hands high up in the air, (raise hands high)
Then down at your side, (hands beside you)
Now touch your hair.
Hold your hands high up as before,
Now you may clap,
One, two, three, four!

HEAD, SHOULDERS, KNEES AND TOES

Head, shoulders, knees, and toes,
Eyes and ears, mouth and nose.
Head and shoulders, knees and toes,
We'll all jump down together. (stoop down)

I'M A PUPPET

I'm a puppet, (dangle arms like a puppet)
On a string.
I can leap, (jump)
And I can spring. (crumple down and then jump up)
I can wave, (wave at friends)
And throw a kiss. (throw a kiss)
I can move, (move around)
My arms like this. (swing arms around)
I can even,
Climb a wall. (pretend to climb a wall)
But....loose my strings,
And I will fall! (fall down)

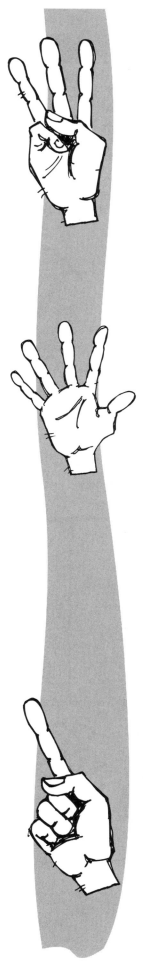

MR. LEFT AND MR. RIGHT

This is Mr. Left. (hold up left thumb)
This is Mr. Right. (hold up right thumb)
They have two little houses just alike. (make fist for houses)
Mr. Left says, "Hi there, How are you tonight?" (wave left thumb)
Mr. Right says, Hello, I'm alright." (wave right thumb)
So arm in arm, off they go, (hook thumbs)
They talk and they walk, First fast and then slow. (move hooked thumbs rapidly and then slowly)
Back they come, and wave good night, (Wave thumbs)
Pop into their houses and are out of sight. (close fingers over thumbs)

MR. TALL AND MR. SMALL

Once there was a man,
Who was tall, tall, tall, (stand on tip-toes)
He had a friend,
Who was small, small, small, (stoop down low)
The man who was small, (stoop)
Would try to call,
To the man who was tall.
"Hello, up there!" (look up, hands to mouth)
The man who was tall, (stand on tip-toes)
At once would call,
To the man who was small.
"Hello, down there!" (look down, hands to mouth)
Then each tipped his hat,
And made this reply:
"Good-bye, my friend." (stoop, look up)
"Good-bye, good-bye."

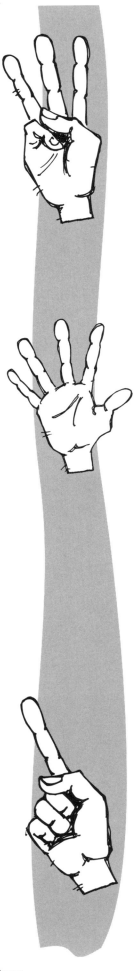

MY BED

I have a little bed just for me, (hands outstretched, palms up)
Brother's too big for it, (measure brother's height)
Mom's too big for it, (measure Mom's height)
Dad's too big for it. (measure Dad's height)
I have a little bed, (hands outstretched, palms up)
But my cat's too small for it, (hand height of cat)
Puppy's too small for it, (hand height of dog)
Baby's too small for it, (hand height of baby)
It's just for me. (pointer fingers on smile)

MY EYES

Here are my eyes, (touch eyes)
One and two, (touch each eye as you say the numbers)
I give a wink, (wink as you say it)
So can you, (point to the child)
When they're open, (hold open with your fingers)
I see the light, (point to the light)
When they're closed, (place fingers on eye lids)
It's dark like night.

MY HANDS

My hands are such good helpers,
In everything I do,
From washing my face and combing my hair, (wash face, comb hair)
To lacing up my shoes. (lace shoes)
I throw a ball and catch a ball, (throw and catch)
And clap my hands this way.
I use my hands so very much,
When I'm at work or play.

RIGHT AND LEFT HANDS

This is my right hand, (raise right hand and wave)
I'll raise it up high.
This is my left hand, (raise left hand and wave it)
I'll touch the sky.
Right hand, left hand, (raise right and then left hands)
Roll them around, (roll them around)
Left hand, right hand, (hold up left and then right)
Pound, pound, pound. (make fist and pound)

STRETCHING

I stretch my arms out far and wide, (stretch arms out)
And whirl them 'round and 'round. (whirl arms around)
Then once more shake my hands and feet, (shake arms and feet)
And then I tumble to the ground. (gently tumble to the ground)

UP AND DOWN

Here we go up, up, up; (stand on tiptoes and reach up high)
Here we go down, down, down; (stoop and touch toes)
Here we go back and forth; (bend back and forth)
Here we go around and around; (turn around twice)
And now we sit right down. (sit down)

USE YOUR EYES

Use your eyes, use your eyes,
You can look and see;
If you have on _____, (call out a color)
Come and stand by me.

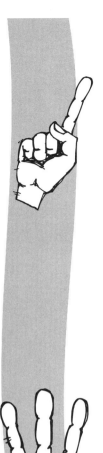
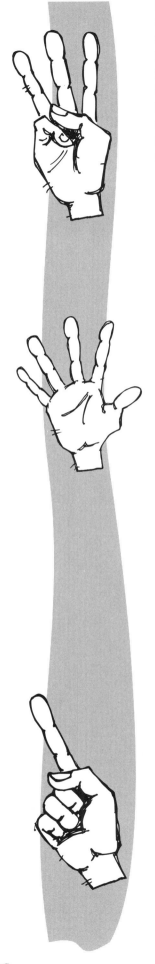

WHAT MY BODY CAN DO

My hands can clap; (clap 3 times)
My feet can tap; (tap toes 3 times)
My eyes can brightly shine. (blink eyes)
My ears can hear; (cup hand to ear)
My nose can smell; (sniff)
My mouth can speak a rhyme. (hands around mouth)

WIGGLE

Wiggle, wiggle, fingers,
Right up to the sky. (wiggle fingers up high)
Wiggle, wiggle, fingers,
Wave them all good-bye. (wave fingers good-bye)
Wiggle, wiggle, fingers,
Right into a ball. (fist together to make ball)
Now throw it in your lap,
And do not let it fall. (throw ball in lap)

PREPARING FOR QUIET TIME

Bible Thoughts

Give thanks to the Lord. Psalm 107:1
I like to go to church. Psalm 122:1
I was glad when they said, "Let us go to church." Psalm 122:1
God gave us ears to hear and eyes to see. Proverbs 20:12
Jesus went to church. Luke 2:27
Pray for one another. James 5:16

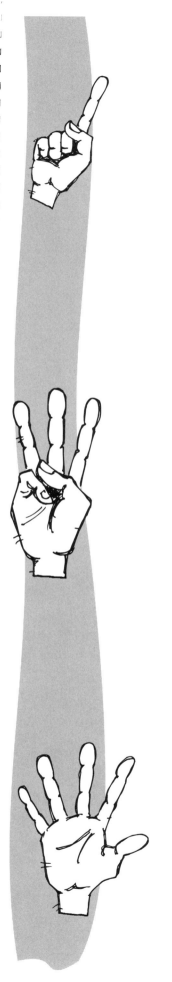
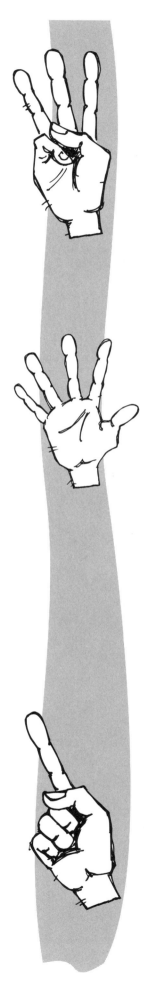

DO THESE MOTIONS

Two little feet go tap, tap, tap,
Two little hands go clap, clap, clap,
One little body jumps up from the chair,
Two little arms stretch high in the air.
Ten little fingers go thump, thump, thump,
Two little feet go jump, jump, jump,
One little body turns around and around,
One little child sits quietly down.

DO THIS

Jump up, jump down,
Everyone turn around.
Look up, look down,
Everyone touch the ground.
Hands up, hands down,
Everyone sits down.
Clap, clap, clap,
Hands in lap.

THE WATCH

I have a little watch, (make circle with thumb and index finger)
Hold it up near your ear, (place circle up to your ear)
Hear it ticking, ticking fast,
It tells us when our playtime's past.

HANDS

Hands on shoulders,
Hands on knees,
Hands in lap,
If you please?

HELLO HANDS

Hello hands, go clap, clap, clap, (clap hands)
Hello feet, go stamp, stamp, stamp, (stamp feet)
Hello teacher, I'll smile at you. (smile)
Hello friend, I'll wave at you. (wave)
Hello body, I'll turn around. (turn around)
Hello chair, I'll sit right down. (sit down)

I TOUCH

I touch my hair, my lips, my eyes, (touch as directed)
I sit up straight, (sit up straight)
And then I rise, (stand)
I touch my nose, my ears, my chin, (touch as directed)
And quietly sit back down again. (sit down)

I WIGGLE

I wiggle my fingers, (wiggle fingers)
I wiggle my toes, (wiggle toes)
I wiggle my shoulders, (wiggle shoulders)
I wiggle my nose. (wiggle nose)
Now there are no more wiggles left in me;
So I am still as still can be. (fold hands in lap)

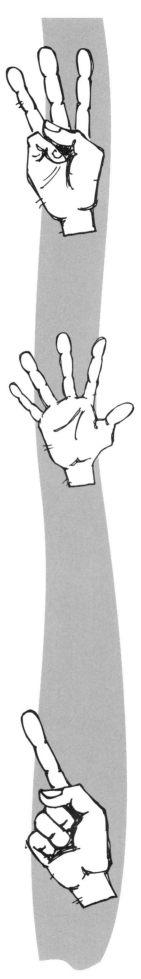

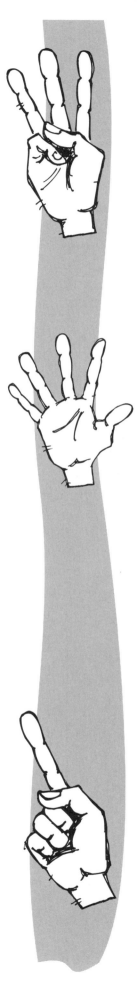

MY FINGERS

I have ten little fingers, (hold up ten fingers)
And they all belong to me.
Would you like to see?
I can shut them up tight, (make a fist)
I can put them together, (fingers together)
Or make them all hide. (put them behind the back)
I can make them move high, (move fingers high)
I can make them move low, (move fingers down)
I can fold them quietly, (fold hands) *
And hold them just so. (hold hands very still)

MY HANDS
(make described motions)

My hands upon my head I place,
Upon my shoulders, on my face,
At my waist and by my side,
And then behind me they will hide.
Then I raise them way up high,
And let my fingers swiftly fly.
Then clap, one, two, three,
And see how quiet they can be.

MY HANDS

Sometimes my hands are by my side, (hands beside side)
Sometimes behind my back they hide, (hands behind back)
Sometimes my hands go clap, clap, clap, (clap hands)
Sometimes I put them in my lap. (hands in lap)
Now they're quiet as can be. (hold hands still in lap)
For it's story time now you see.

OPEN SHUT THEM

Open, shut them, Open, shut them,
Give a little clap,
Open, shut them, open, shut them,
Lay them in your lap.

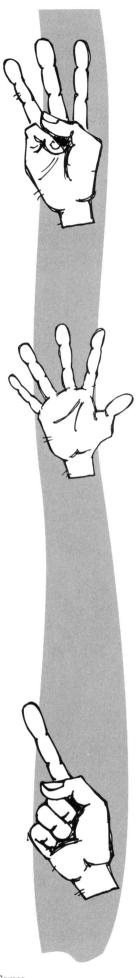

SH...SH...SH...SHHH

Make one eye go wink, wink, wink. (Wink one eye)
Make two eyes go blink, blink, blink. (Blink both eyes)
Make two fingers stand just so, (Hold up two fingers)
Then ten fingers in a row. (Hold up ten fingers)
Front and back your head will rock, (Head back and forth)
Then your fist will knock, knock, knock. (Thump fist together)
Stretch and make a yawn so wide, (stretch and yawn)
Drop you arms down to your sides. (let arms fall)
Close your eyes and help me say, (Close eyes)
Our very quiet sound today. (sh..sh..sh..shhhh)

TOUCH EXERCISE

I'll touch my hair, my lips, my eyes,
I'll sit up straight, and then I'll rise,
I'll touch my ears, my nose, my chin,
Then quietly sit down again.

TWO LITTLE HANDS

Two little hands go clap, clap, clap. (clap hands)
Two little feet go tap, tap, tap. (tap toes)
Two little hands go thump, thump, thump. (pound fingers on one
hand in palm of other hand)
Two little feet go jump, jump, jump. (jump up and down)
One little body turns around, (turn around)
And one little child sits quietly down. (sit down, quietly)

WIGGLES

I wiggle my fingers,
I wiggle my toes,
I wiggle my shoulders,
I wiggle my nose.
Now no more wiggles are left in me,
So I will be still as I can be.

 DOVE

 EAGLE

 FISH

 JONAH

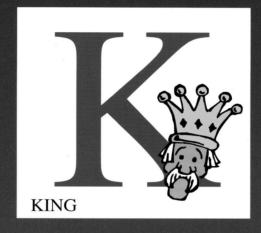 KING

 LAMB

 PRAY

 QUEEN

 RAIN

 VINE

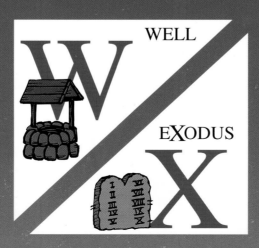 WELL

EXODUS

 YOKE

ZEBRA

RECIPES

Preparing a recipe is a wonderful experience for a preschool. It reinforces so many skills: small muscle development, analytical skills, cognitive skills, following directions, and nutrition. The following recipes are simple enough to prepare in the classroom by the children with some guidance by the teacher. This can also be used as a time to talk to the children about the Bible lesson you are teaching that day as well as God's love and care for us.

Bible Thoughts

God made plants with seed. Genesis 1:11
Everything God made was very good. Genesis 1:31
Think about the wonderful things God made. Job 37:14
God loves us. Psalm 107:1
God gives food to us. Psalm 136:25
God gives food to animals. Psalm 147:9
We are helpers. 2 Corinthians 1:24
God cares for you. 1 Peter 5:7

ANTS ON A LOG

Materials: Celery, peanut butter, raisins, place setting knives, paper towels

Guidance: Before the session, clean and cut the celery into 4 inch pieces. Allow the children to spread the peanut butter on the celery (filling the groove), and sprinkle the raisins on it.

APPLE ICE CREAM SODA

Materials: Apple juice, vanilla ice cream, ginger ale, plastic glasses, straws, teaspoons

Guidance: Place a scoop of ice cream in each cup. Let each child pour 1/2 cup apple juice over the ice cream. Let him stir it. Now fill the

BANANA TREATS

Materials: Bananas, toothpicks, wheat germ, small paper plates, forks, place setting knife, spoon

Guidance: As the children arrive in the center, give them a small plate. Let them spoon a small amount of wheat germ on their plate. Give each of the children a half of a banana and tell them to slice it with the knife. Using a toothpick, they may pick up a slice, dip it into the wheat germ, and eat it. Talk to the children about eating healthy snacks.

BUTTER

Materials: Baby food jars, whipping cream, salt, crackers, paper plates

Guidance: Pour some of the whipping cream in several jars. Screw the lid on tightly. Give a jar to several of the children. Tell them to shake it for a long time. If they become tired you may need to finish shaking it. It will become thick and stick to the sides of the jar, and then it will form a yellow ball inside with white liquid around it. The yellow is the butter. Remove the butter and place it on a paper plate. Add a little salt. If you desire it to be a little firmer you may refrigerate it for a little while. Let the children spread it on crackers and eat it. Be sure to tell them where cream comes from.

BUTTERSCOTCH CEREAL BARS

Materials: Mixing bowl, serving spoon, 9X9X2 pan (greased), butterscotch chips, light corn syrup, margarine, vanilla, Cherrios™, marshmallows, microwave oven

1 cup butterscotch chips
1/2 cup light corn syrup
2 Tablespoons margarine
1 teaspoon vanilla
1 1/2 cup miniature marshmallows
5 cups Cherrios™

Guidance: Grease the pan and set it aside. Place the butterscotch chips, corn syrup, margarine, and vanilla in the bowl and microwave until the chips are completely melted. Be careful not to over heat. Stir in the cereal and marshmallows and mix well until the cereal is well coated. Press in the pan. Cool.

CELERY, STUFFED

Materials: Celery, deviled ham, place setting knives, small plates

Guidance: Before the session, wash and cut the celery into pieces. Give each of the children a piece of celery. Let them fill the celery with the deviled ham. Eat.

CHOCOLATE PUDDING DONUTS

Materials: Mixing bowls, beater, tablespoons, teaspoons, individual serving dishes, paper towel, donuts, chocolate instant pudding, milk

Guidance: Let the children help to make the pudding. Allow a few minutes for it to thicken. Give each child a donut to go in the bottom of their dish. Let each child dip chocolate pudding and put it on the top of their donut. Eat and enjoy.

CINNAMON APPLE SLICES

Materials: Cinnamon, sugar, apples, baking sheet, foil, container, peeler, knife, oven
1 teaspoon cinnamon
1 Tablespoon sugar
2 baking apples

Guidance: Peel, core, and slice the apples. Mix the cinnamon with the sugar. Spread the apple slices in a single layer on the baking sheet. Let the children sprinkle the cinnamon mixture over the apples slices. Cover the baking sheet with the foil. Bake at 350 degrees for 10 to 20 minutes or until the apples are soft. Cool and serve.

COCOA KRISPIES™ BALLS

Materials: Mixing bowl, mixing spoon, measuring cup, waxed paper, peanut butter, corn syrup, Cocoa Krispies™, sugar, powdered sugar, cookie sheet
1/2 cup peanut butter
1/2 cup light corn syrup
2 cups Cocoa Krispies™
1 cup confectioners sugar

Guidance: Let the children help pour the ingredients into the bowl as you mix them together. When the cereal is well coated, spoon the mixture onto a piece of waxed paper. Allow the children to make a ball of the mixture. Tell them to drop the ball into the container of powdered sugar and roll it around. Place the balls on a cookie sheet until they are firm.

COTTAGE CHEESE DIP

Materials: Cottage cheese, sugar (or honey), rippled potato chips, paper plates, teaspoons, serving spoons.

Guidance: Let each child spoon some cottage cheese on his plate. Let him sprinkle it with sugar. Tell him to stir the mixture. Let him use the chips to dip the mixture and eat it.

CRANANA FROSTY

Materials: Cranberry juice, orange juice, ice cubes, bananas, blender (or food processor), small cups, place setting knives, teaspoons
2 cups cranberry juice
2/3 cup orange juice
10 ice cubes
1 cup bananas, sliced

Guidance: Combine the cranberry juice, orange juice, ice cubes, and 1/2 cup sliced bananas in the blender. Process until smooth. Pour the mixture into small cups and top with the remaining banana slices. Let the children eat the frosty with a spoon. Makes 6 - 1/2 cup servings.

DELICIOUS DIP

Materials: Cottage cheese, cheddar cheese, dill, Worcestershire sauce, salt, container, spoon, fork
1 cup low fat cottage cheese
1/3 cup grated cheddar cheese
1 teaspoon dried dill
2 teaspoon Worcestershire sauce
1/2 teaspoon salt

Guidance: Mix the cottage cheese with the cheddar cheese. Add the dill, Worcestershire, and salt. Mash the mixture with a fork until it is smooth. Serve with raw vegetables. Makes 1 1/3 cups.

DIRT PUDDING

Materials: Instant chocolate pudding, Oreos™, milk, food processor, individual serving dishes, teaspoons

Guidance: Mix chocolate pudding according to directions on the box. Put the Oreos™ in a food processor and process until they are crumbs. Let the children spoon some pudding into their dish and sprinkle the crumbs over the pudding. Serve.

FRUIT KABOB

Materials: Oranges, apples, grapes, bananas, pineapple, cheese cubes, skewers

Guidance: Before the session, make a kabob using the fruit and cheese. Let the children see if they can copy the pattern you have made. Allow them to eat their fruit and then make a pattern of their own and eat it.

GRAPE PUNCH

Materials: Grape juice, ginger ale, ice cubes, glasses

Guidance: Let each of the children place two ice cubes in their glass, and pour 1/4 cup grape juice in. Fill the remaining space with ginger ale. Drink and enjoy.

HONEY YUMS

Materials: Peanut butter, powdered sugar, rice cereal, honey, raisins, bowl, mixing spoon, measuring cup
1/2 cup peanut butter
1/2 cup powdered sugar
1/2 cup crispy rice cereal
1/2 cup honey
1/2 cup raisins

Guidance: Pour each of the ingredients into a bowl. Mix them well. Let the children form balls with the mixture and eat them.

ICE CREAM CONE CUPCAKES

Materials: cake mix (mixed according to directions), ice cream cones, muffin pans, serving spoons, icing

Guidance: Let the children spoon the cake mixture into the cone to about half full and place it in the muffin pan. Place the pans in the oven and bake 350 degree until a tooth pick inserted in the cake comes out clean. Allow to the cones to cool. Let the children ice the cupcakes and eat them.

ICE CREAM FLOAT

Materials: Coke, vanilla ice cream, ice cream scoop, glasses, teaspoons, straws

Guidance: Place a scoop of ice cream in the glass. Let the child, slowly pour in the coke. Tell him to stir a little. Drink.

IRONED SANDWICHES

Materials: Bread, sliced cheese, knives, spoons, heavy foil, iron, soft margarine

Guidance: Have the children place a slice of cheese on the bread and top it with another piece of bread. Let them spread small amounts of margarine on the bread. When they have finished, give them a piece of foil and tell them to wrap their sandwich in the foil. Assisting them, being very careful, help them to iron their sandwich. You will need to flip it over with a spatula, being careful not to burn yourself. Let them iron the other side of the sandwich. Allow it to cool a few minutes before they unwrap it and eat it.

KABOBS

Materials: Straws, marshmallows, thick slices of bananas, pineapple slices.

Guidance: Give each of the children a straw, marshmallows, bananas slices, and pineapple slices. Dip the end of the straw in water and let the child alternate the marshmallows and fruit, starting with a marshmallow and ending with one.

LEMONADE

Materials: Lemons, lemon squeezer, pitcher, sugar, water, serving spoon, glasses

Guidance: Let the children help to squeeze the lemons. Pour some water in the pitcher and add sugar. Let the children help to stir the mixture until the sugar is dissolved. Add lemon juice and stir it well. Serve.

OATMEAL COOKIES (NO-BAKE)

Materials: Margarine, powdered sugar, water, oatmeal, cocoa, vanilla, mixing bowl, spatula, waxed paper

1 cup margarine
1 cup powdered sugar
2 Tablespoons water
2 1/2 cup oatmeal (uncooked)

4 Tablespoons cocoa
1 teaspoon vanilla
1/4 cup powdered sugar

Guidance: Allow the children to help to mix the ingredient together. Give each child a piece of waxed paper. Spoon a mound of the mixture onto the paper. Let the children make a ball and then roll it in the powdered sugar. Let them eat their cookies.

PANCAKE JELLY ROLLS

Materials: Pancakes, jelly, small plates, plastic knives, spoon

Guidance: Before the session, cook or purchase the pancakes. Spoon some jelly on the top of each of the children's pancake. Let him spread the jelly. Tell him to start on the side and roll the pancake up. When it is rolled up tell him to eat it.

PEANUT BUTTER (HOMEMADE)

Materials: Peanuts, honey, vegetable oil, container, blender, crackers, place setting knives, small plates

Guidance: Let the children help to shell the peanuts and put them in the blender. Add a small amount of honey and blend. If the mixture seems dry add a little vegetable oil and blend again. Give each child a plate and let them spread the peanut butter on the crackers and eat it.

PEANUT BUTTER BALLS

Materials: Peanut butter, powdered sugar, margarine, rice cereal, container, spoon, measuring cup

1 cup peanut butter
1 1/2 cup powdered sugar
1/2 stick margarine (soft)
2 cups rice cereal

Guidance: Let the children help measure the ingredients and pour them into the container. Help them mix the mixture well. Place a spoonful of the mixture on waxed paper for each child and let them form a ball. Allow them to eat it.

PEANUT BUTTER PLAYDOUGH

Materials: Powdered sugar, flour, peanut butter, measuring cup, mixing bowl, spoon, waxed paper

1 cup powdered sugar

1 cup flour

2 cups peanut butter

Guidance: Put the peanut butter in the bowl and gradually add the powdered sugar and flour. Stir well. Knead. Place on a floured surface. Let the children play and eat the dough.

PICKLE POP

Materials: Large dill pickle, small craft sticks

Guidance: Help the child to push the stick into the pickle. Tell him to hold the stick and eat the pickle.

PIZZA ON A BUN

Materials: Hamburger buns, pizza quick sauce, sliced cheese, baking pan, teaspoons, oven

Guidance: Give each child a top or bottom of the bun. Tell them to place a spoonful of the sauce on it and spread it around. Place a slice of cheese on it. Place the bun on a cookie sheet and place it in the oven and bake at 350 degrees until it is melted.

SESAME CRACKERS

Materials: Whole-wheat flour, soy flour, sesame seeds, salt, oil, water, container, spoon, baking sheet, rolling pen

1 1/2 cups whole-wheat flour

1/4 cup soy flour

1/4 cup sesame seeds

1 teaspoon salt

1/4 cup vegetable oil

1/2 cup water

Guidance: Stir together the flours, sesame seed, and salt. Add the oil and blend well. Add water gradually, until the mixture is all wet and sticking together. Roll out to 1/4 inch thick and cut into sticks. Bake on an ungreased baking sheet at 350 degrees until crisp, approximately 10 minutes. Makes 3 dozen crackers.

SHAPE SANDWICHES

Materials: Shape cookie cutters, bread, container, filling, place setting knives, tablespoons

Guidance: Before the session, mix up the filling you plan to use. Allow the children to spread the filling on the bread and place another piece of bread on top. You can cut off the ends and place them in a plastic bag. Give the children the cookie cutters and tell them to press it hard onto the sandwich (make sure it cuts all the way through). Allow them to eat the shape and the "scraps." Save the ends and take them outside to feed to the birds at recess.

STIR-FRIED VEGETABLES

Materials: Cooking oil, green peppers, red peppers, onions, carrots, celery, broccoli, pea pods, mushrooms, soy sauce, wok, small paper saucers, plastic spoons or forks

Guidance: This activity requires very close supervision but can be a fun experience. This is a good activity to teach children about "children around the world." Bring the food items into the classroom already prepared for cooking. Allow the children to pour the food into the wok, plug it in, and cook the vegetables. Allow the children to taste the different flavors.

S'MORES

Materials: Graham crackers, chocolate frosting, tiny marshmallows, plastic knives, napkins, small plates

Guidance: Give each of the children a plate, two crackers, marshmallows, and a knife. Allow each of the children to spread the frosting on the crackers. Place the marshmallows on one of the crackers and cover them with the other cracker. Eat.

STRAWBERRY BALLS

Materials: Strawberry gelatin, condensed milk, coconut, container
4 small packages strawberry gelatin
1 can condensed milk
1 can coconut
red decorator sugar

Guidance: In the container, mix together the ingredients. cover and refrigerate until ready to form the balls. Form the balls and roll them in red decorator sugar. The balls are now ready to eat.

SNACKS (COLORS)

BLACK SNACKS

Raisins
Dewberries
Blackberries

BLUE SNACKS

Blueberries

BROWN SNACKS

Wieners (sliced)
Hershey Kisses™
Cocoa Krispies™
Chocolate pudding

GREEN SNACKS

Green Bell Peppers
Green Apples
Celery
Lettuce
Lime gelatin
Broccoli
Green seedless grapes
Pickles
Honey Dew Melon

ORANGE SNACKS

Oranges
Cantaloupe
Carrots
Orange gelatin

PURPLE SNACKS

Purple seedless grapes
Purple Plums
Grape gelatin

RED SNACKS

Apples
Kidney beans (washed and drained)
Ketchup
Red peppers
Cranberry Juice
Tomatoes
Salsa
Cherries
Beets
Raspberries
Cranberry juice
Watermelon

YELLOW SNACKS

Cheese Cubes
Lemon pudding
Bananas
Pineapple
Yellow squash

WHITE SNACKS

Marshmallows
Popcorn
Cucumber slices (peeled)

GAMES

Children love games. An organized playtime is a wonderful way to run off excess energy and a good reinforcement tool for different teaching concepts. Use this as an opportunity to remind the children of the Bible thought you may be teaching that day.

Bible Thoughts

God called the light day and the darkness He called night. Genesis 1:5
God made the animals. Genesis 1:25
Everything God made was very good. Genesis 1:31
God is good to us. Psalm 73:1
God made us. Psalm 100:3
I am wonderfully made. Psalm 139:14
A friend loves at all times. Proverbs 17:17
God made the world. Acts 17:24
Be kind one to another. Ephesians 4:32
Love one another. 1 John 4:7

AUTOMOBILES

Materials: Chalk

Guidance: Draw a very large circle on the sidewalk or gym floor. Tell the children to stand on the line and then face counterclockwise (you will need to explain since they do not know the term). On the signal "Go" everyone runs around the circle pretending to be a automobile. They may pass each other on the left, but they may not reverse directions of running. When the whistle blows, all automobiles must stop, stop any noise, and look at the instructor. Those failing to do so, or those who bump into another automobile must go to a garage (a designated area) for repairs. This is an interesting way for children to respond quickly to the whistle or verbal signal from the instructor. A variation can be for the instructor to add a stop sign or other traffic rules to the game.

BIRD CATCHER

Materials: None

Guidance: Before beginning the game, select one of the children to be the mother bird and select two or three of the children to be bird catchers. Divide the remaining children into kinds of birds (blue birds, black birds, robins, and etc.). In one corner of the room there is a cage and in another corner of the room there is a bird nest. The mother bird is in her nest in one corner of the room. The bird catchers stand between the nest and the cage. When the mother calls out, bluebirds, all the bluebirds fly for the nest. The bird catchers try to tag them. If they are tagged, they go to the cage. If he gets to the nest before he is tagged, he is safe. The game continues until all the kinds of birds have been called and then the game begins again.

COOPERATIVE CARRY

Materials: beach balls, towels

Guidance: Tell the children to choose partners. Give each team a towel and tell them to hold the corners. Place the ball on each teams towel and tell them to travel around the round the room without dropping the ball. To make the game more difficult, tell them to make the ball bounce each time you clap your hands.

FOOD MEMORY MATCHING GAME

Materials: Pictures of food, poster board, glue, clear contact

Guidance: Cut 2 identical pictures from magazines, coupon section of the paper or labels from cans. Glue them on squares cut from poster board. Laminate them. To play the game, tell the children to turn all the cards over with the food picture face down. Have a child turn up one of the cards and then see if he can match it with another identical card. If he matches the cards, he get to keep trying until he misses. If he does not match, it is then the next child's turn.

GROCERY STORE GAME

Materials: Construction paper, pictures of food items, glue, clear adhesive plastic

Guidance: Tell the children to stand in a large circle. Give each child a picture of the food items. The teacher walks around the circle saying: "I went to the grocery store and I bought some _____ (name a food item that one of the children has). The child with that food item then follows the teacher. She continues the process until all the food items have been named and all the children are following the teacher. She then says: "And then I went home." The children then return to their places. After playing the game you may wish for one of the children to be the leader.

I SAW

Materials: None

Guidance: Have all the children stand in a circle and choose one child to be the leader. Tell the child to march around the circle, and then stop in front of one of the children. He then ask, "What did you see?" He then does the action (a horse galloping, a lion roaring, a man mowing, and etc.) while the other children try to guess what it is. The child who guesses correctly becomes the leader.

I SPY (Myself Unit)

Materials: Select one of the children to be the leader. Tell him to describe one of the children in the class without looking at him. The other children try to guess who the person is. The one who guesses becomes the leader.

I SPY (COMMUNITY HELPERS)

Materials: Pictures of community helpers.

Guidance: Before the session, place the pictures around the room. Choose one of the children to be the leader. Tell him to describe (without looking at it) one of the community helpers in one of the pictures. Let the other children guess who the helper is. The one who guesses, becomes the leader.

I SPY (FARM ANIMALS)

Materials: Pictures of farm animals.

Guidance: Before the session, place the pictures around the room. Choose one of the children to be the leader. Tell him to describe (without looking at it) one of the farm animals and let the other children try to guess which animal he has described. The one who guesses, become the leader.

I SPY (ZOO ANIMALS)

Materials: Pictures of zoo animals.

Guidance: Before the session, place the pictures around the room. Choose one of the children to be the leader. Tell him to describe (without looking at it) one of the zoo animals and let the other children try to guess which animal he has described. The one who guesses, becomes the leader.

LISTENING GAME

Materials: None

Guidance: Tell the children that you are going to count to three, and then clap. When you clap, everyone must sit still and quiet until you clap again (about 30 seconds). Tell them to listen while they are sitting still and quiet. When you clap the second time, call on one of the children to tell what they heard while being quiet. Call on the children until all have had a chance to tell you what they heard.

MIDNIGHT

Materials: None

Guidance: Select one of the children to be Mother Hen and another child to be the Mr. Fox. The chickens, at one end of the play space called the chicken coop, follow Mother Hen up to Mr. Fox, who stands in his den 20 to 30 yards away. Mother Hen asks Mr. Fox, "What time is it Mr. Fox?" Mr. Fox looks at his watch and answers any time he chooses. When he answers "Midnight!" Mother Hen and the chickens run back to the coop with Mr. Fox chasing after them. Those tagged by Mr. Fox become his helpers. To discourage children from permitting themselves to be tagged, stress the fact that those who are not tagged are the best runners.

MOTHER CAT AND KITTENS

Materials: None

Guidance: Use the following poem:

> Mother cat and kittens were fast asleep one day.
> The mother wanted to sleep, but the kittens wanted to play.
> So, they got up, oh, so quietly and walked away.

Choose a child to the be mother cat. Act out the verse. While the mother cat sleeps the kittens hide in the room. When the mother cat wakes up she hunts the kittens. When they are found they return to the circle.

PARTNER, PARTNER

Materials: None

Guidance: Tell each child to choose a partner. Tell them that you will name an action and each set of partners can do the action. Say:
Put your feet together.
Put your elbows together.
Put your ears together.
Put your shoulders together.
Put your hands together.
After a few actions have been done, tell the children to choose a different partner.

POLICEMAN, POLICEMAN

Materials: None

Guidance: Have all the children make a large circle. Choose one of the children to be the policeman. One of the children in the circle will say "Mr. Policeman, Mr. Policeman, I have lost my child. Do you think you can help me find him?" The "policeman" answers him "yes." He then describes to the policeman, what his child is wearing (he describes one of the children in the circle without looking at him). The policeman then tries to find the child that was described. You may also want to add another dimension to this game by going to one of the children and ask other questions that pertain to police work. Ask questions like: how long have you been a policeman? How do you find lost children? How do you talk to the station while you are in you police car? and etc.

POTATO HOP

Materials: Brown construction paper, scissors, tape

Guidance: Cut 10 large potato shapes out of the brown construction paper and number them 1 to 10. Tape the shapes to the floor in numerical order. Let the children take turns hopping from one potato to another as everyone chants the following rhyme.
One potato, two potato, three potato, four,
Five potato, six potato, and I want some more.
Seven potato, eight potato, I really love 'em.
Nine potato, ten potato, bake 'em in the oven.

RACING IN A CIRCLE

Materials: None

Guidance: Tell all the children to stand in a circle. One child is chosen to be "it." "It" walks around the circle and stops and points between two of the children. Those two child run in different directions around the circle and return to their place. The first one back becomes "it" and the game begins again.

RAILROAD TRAIN

Materials: Concrete chalk

Guidance: Draw a long straight line on the concrete. Give each child the name of a car of a train (engine, coal car, passenger car, freight car, caboose, and etc.). The teacher will probably have to be the engineer, depending on the age of the children. The engineer calls the names of the cars. The children run and stand on the line. When all the "cars" have joined the train the engineer says, "Toot-toot" and the train starts off on a trip.

ROOMS FOR RENT

Materials: Chalk

Guidance: A child is chosen to be "it." All the other children stand in a circle and an "X" is made where each one is standing. The child who is chosen as "it" goes around the circle and ask various player "Any rooms to rent?" The answer is "No." While the child is trying to find a room to rent the other children may swap rooms behind him. If he is able to get in a room as they move the child that is left out becomes "it." If he is unable to find a room, he can say, "Moving Day" and all the children must move into another room and he tries to get one of the rooms. The left out player becomes "it."

RHYMING WORDS

Materials: Rhymes

Guidance: Say the rhyme and have the children fill in the black with a rhyming word.

> Pitter, pitter, pat
> The rain fell on my _____(hat).
>
> Out in the sun,
> See me _____(run).
>
> Run, play, sing
> Today is _____(spring).
>
> Munch, munch, crunch,
> I am eating _____(lunch).
>
> Come here and look,
> Please read this _____(book).

RHYTHM GAME

Materials: Drum (homemade or purchased)

Guidance: Tell the children to move to the beat of the drum. Include rhythms such as: walking, running, skipping, tiptoeing, and stomping.

RINGMASTER

Materials: None

Guidance: Select one child to be the ringmaster. The other children sit in a circle. The ringmaster moves around the circle and selects each child in turn to perform as a circus animal. The other children try to guess what the animal is. If they are unable to guess, the child tells them what the animal is. When the ringmaster calls "lets join the parade," all the children stand and march around the circle.

SHAPE MATCHING

Materials: Shapes cut out of construction paper, feely box (or bag)

Guidance: Have one of the children come up and pull one of the shapes out of the box. Tell him to find something in the room that is the same shape (or color). Continue until all the children have had a turn.

SNIFF A WHIFF

Materials: Empty film cans, cotton, lemon, banana, onion, orange, chocolate, cinnamon

Guidance: Place the smelling items in the bottom of each can and place a piece of cotton over it. Close the bottle for a few minutes, to give the fragrance time to permeate the can. Open the can and have one of the children smell and see if he can name the fragrance. Replace the cap, and continue letting the children identify the fragrance.

SQUIRREL IN TREES

Materials: None

Guidance: Choose one of the children to be it. Divide the children into groups of three. Two of the children are to join hands to form a "tree." One child stands between the joined hands. When a child in the center calls "change trees," the squirrels must find another tree. Two squirrels cannot be in the same tree. The person in the center tries to find a tree, and leave another child out. That child will become "it." Keep changing persons to be the trees and squirrels until all the children have had a chance to be the squirrel.

STONE GAME

Materials: 2 ropes

Guidance: Each of the ropes are to be stretched out like a goal on opposite ends of the playing area. One child is chosen to be the "stone." All the other children stand in a circle with the "stone" sitting in the center. The "stone" can jump up any time as the other children skip around the circle. When the "stone" jumps up the children run to one of the goals, as the "stone" tries to catch them. If anyone is caught they also become a "stone" and sit in the center. All the "stones" then chase the other children and try to catch them, but no "stone" can move until the first stone moves. The game is over when all the children have been caught.

TALL AND SMALL

Materials: None

Guidance: Players sit in a circle. One of the children is chosen to be in the center. He covers his eyes. Another child is chosen to be the leader. The children say the following poem:
I'm very, very tall
I'm very, very small
Sometimes tall, sometimes small
Guess what I am now?
The leader either stands up tall or squats down small. The child guesses. If he is correct he becomes the leader, if not he stays in the center.

TEASE THE BEAR

Materials: concrete chalk

Guidance: Draw a very large circle on the floor or concrete. One child is chosen as the "bear" and another is chosen as the "bear keeper." All the other children are players. When the "keeper" calls out, "my bear is free!" the children enter the circle and try to tag the "bear" without the keeper tagging them. The "bear" must sit at all times but can help save himself by tagging players before they tag him. If a player is successful in tagging the "bear," he then becomes the "bear" and the other child becomes a player.

THIS IS THE WAY WE HELP AT HOME

Materials: None

Guidance: Select one of the children to be the leader. Sing the song "This is the way we help at home" to the tune of "Mulberry Bush." Let the leader play out an action about home and see if the other children can guess what the child is doing. Give all the children a turn if they so desire.

TURKEY WALK

Materials: None

Guidance: Tell all the children to stoop down and grasp their ankles with their hands. In this position, walk around the room. Tell them when they hear a "gobble, gobble" they are to are to return to their places. When they are in their places, they say "gobble, gobble."

WAYS WE CAN GET THERE

Materials: None

Guidance: Tell the children that you are going to tell them to move from one place to another. Tell them that there are many ways you can get from one place to another. They may choose to: walk, run, creep, fly like a airplane, waddle like a duck, tramp like an elephant, and etc. You may want to allow them to suggest ways, before the game begins. Give them the destination and watch their many different kinds of movement.

WHAT IS MISSING?

Materials: 5 to 7 objects (can be seasonal or other unit items)

Guidance: Have the children sit in a circle. Place the objects in front of you and discuss the names of the objects. Have the children close their eyes and you will remove one of the objects. The children then guess what is missing. You may want to select one of the children to remove one of the objects while the other children close or hide their eyes.

WHO AM I? (FAMILY)

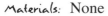

Materials: None

Guidance: Describe members of a family and let the children guess who the people are.

I'm big and tall,
My voice is gruff,
I work very hard,
My whiskers are rough
Who am I?
(Daddy)

When your parents leave
And are gone for a while
I stay with you
And you make me smile
Who am I?
(Babysitter)

I sometimes visit you,
You visit me on a summer day,
I think up games
That you love to play.
Who am I?
(Grandparent)

When I grow up,
You wont call me mister,
Because I'm a girl,
You call me _____.
(Sister)

When I get big
I'll never be a mother
But I may be a dad,
Because I'm your _____.
(Brother)

I like to cook
Or read you a book,
And if you skin your knee,
You may run to me.
Who am I?
(Mother)

WHO HAS THE PENNIES

Materials: Three pennies

Guidance: Select one of the children to be "it." He hides his eyes while the other children pass the three pennies around the group. Upon an agreed signal, "it" opens his eyes and tries to guess who has the pennies. If "it" guesses correctly, the child holding the pennies becomes "it."

WHO IS MISSING?

Materials: Large box (or umbrella), sheet

Guidance: Tell all the children to close their eyes. When all their eyes are closed you will select a child to get inside the box and cover him with the sheet. The other children then try to see if they can guess "Who Is Missing?" If the children have trouble guessing who is missing, give a hint such as: "The missing person is wearing a red dress."
This game can also be used as a "behind the umbrella game" or "who has left the room game."

WOLF

Materials: None

Guidance: One of the children is chosen to be the wolf and he tries to catch the other children. He turns his back to the other children.
Children: "Wolf, wolf, are you ready?
Wolf: No, I have to _____(comb my hair, wash my face, etc.)
Children: "Wolf, wolf, are you ready?"
When the wolf is ready he gives no excuse but turns and runs to catch the children. If one is caught, he sits out until a new game begins.

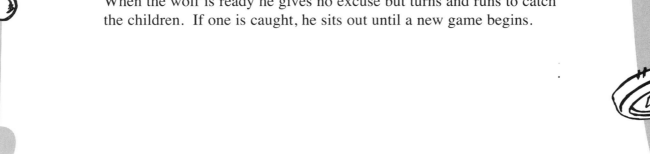